Harry Potter

AND THE
HALF-BLOOD
PRINCE

Selections from

BIG NOTE PIANO

Music by NICHOLAS HOOPER
Arranged by Carol Matz

CONTENTS

Alfred

alfred.com

ISBN-10: 0-7390-6211-5
ISBN-13: 978-0-7390-6211-1

IN NOCTEM

By Nicholas Hooper
Arranged by Carol Matz

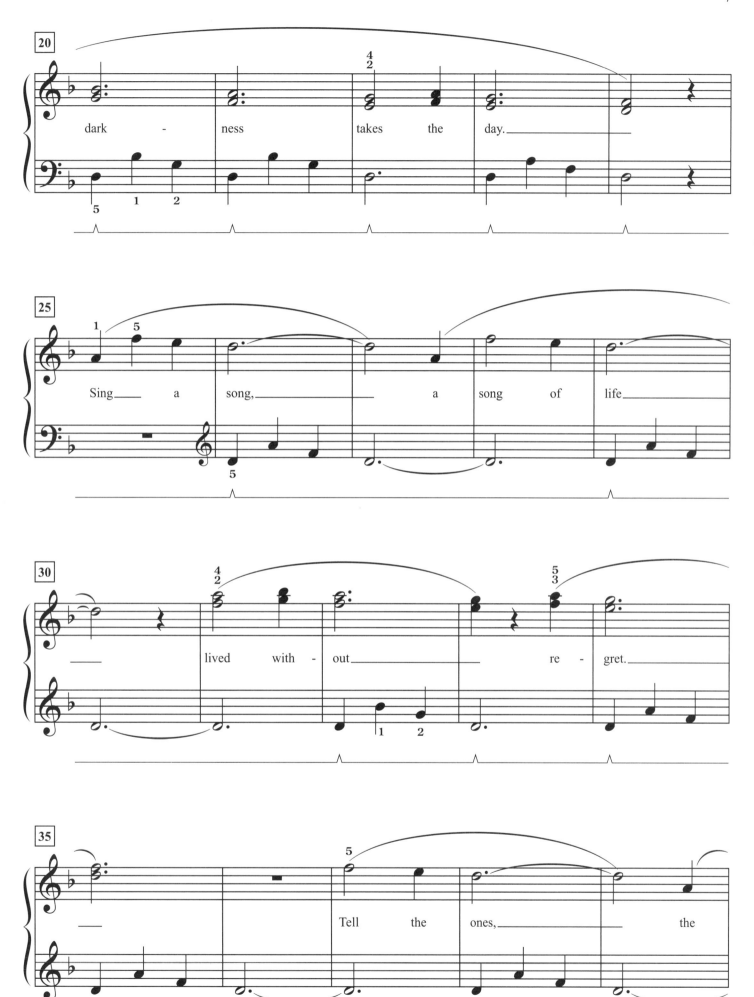

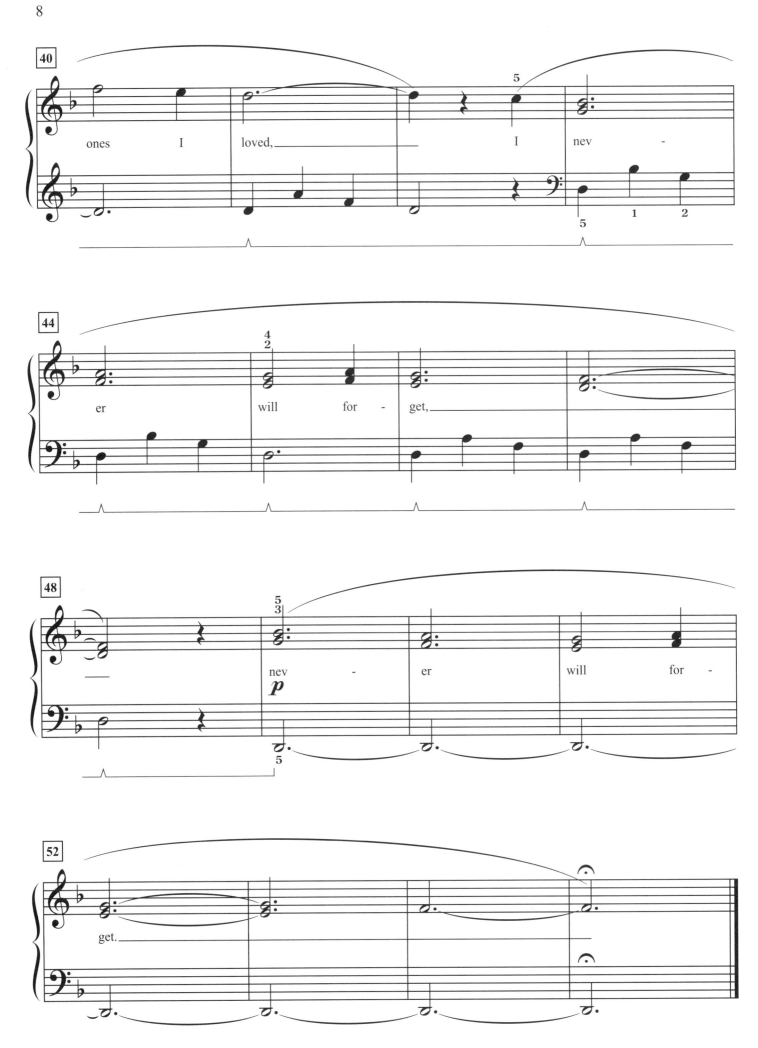

GINNY

By Nicholas Hooper
Arranged by Carol Matz

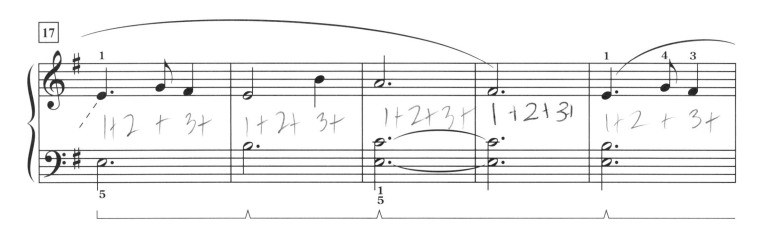

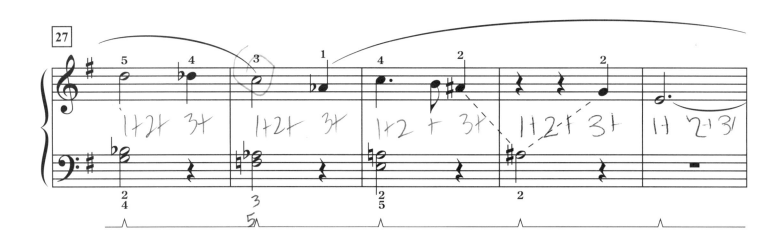

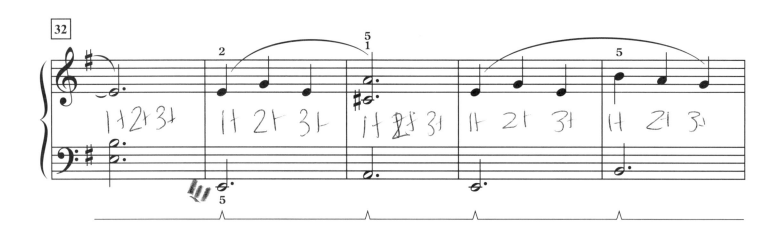

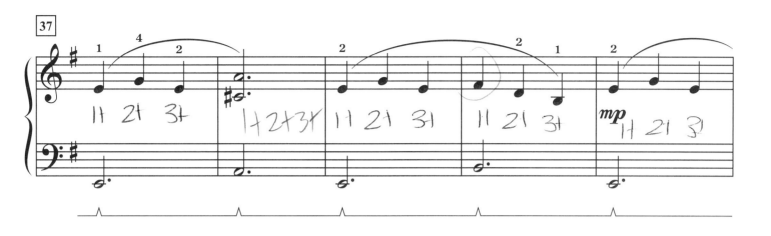

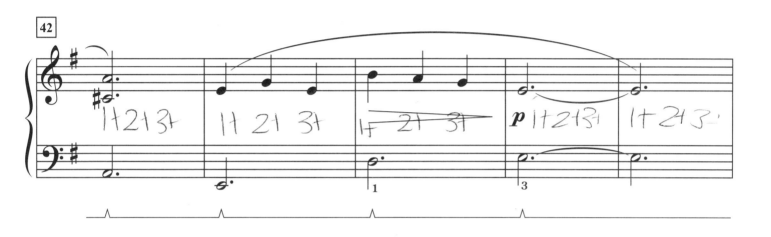

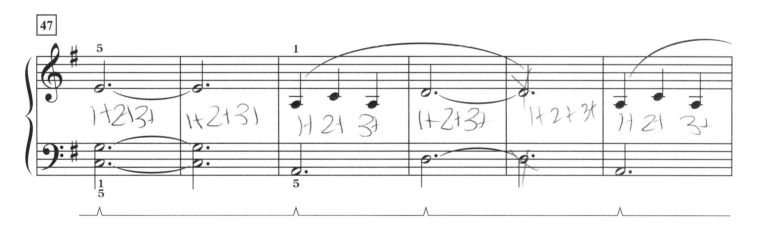

fade away

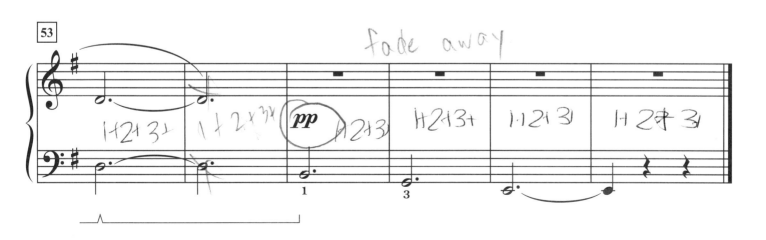

WIZARD WHEEZES

By Nicholas Hooper
Arranged by Carol Matz

Fast swing (♫ = ♩³♪)

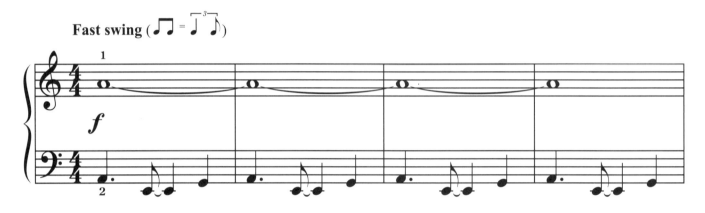

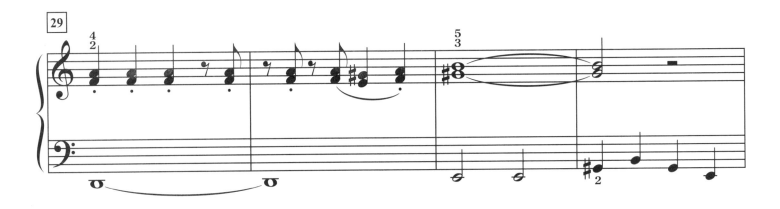

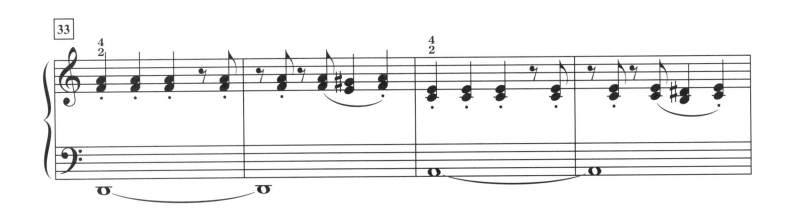

to Coda ⊕

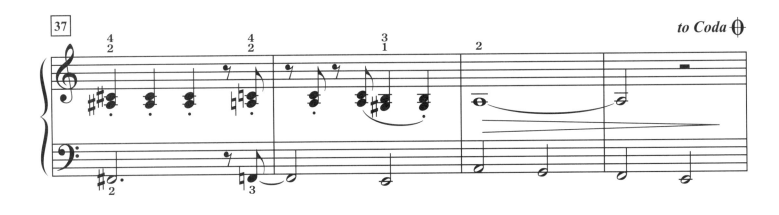

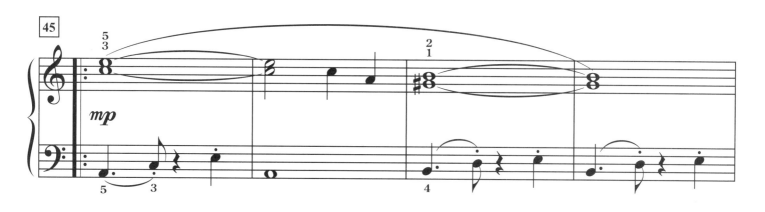

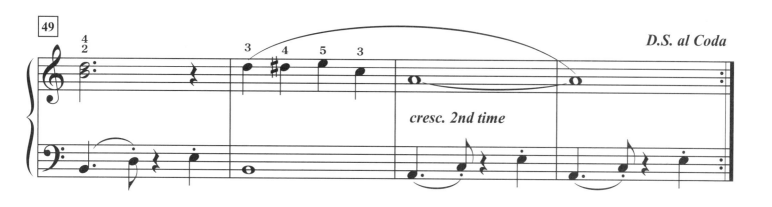

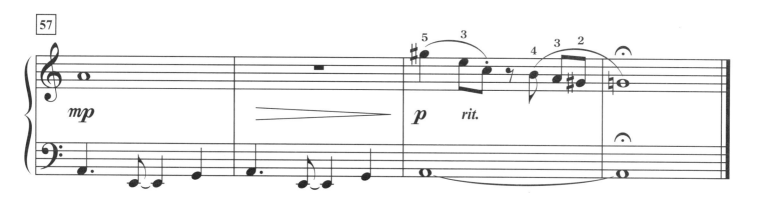

HARRY AND HERMIONE

By Nicholas Hooper
Arranged by Carol Matz

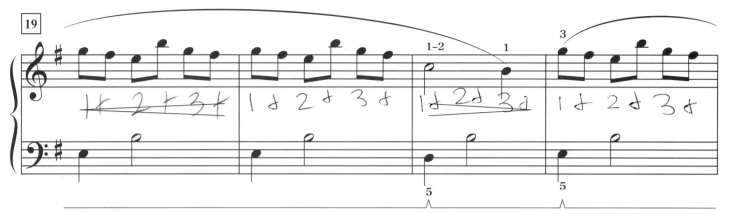

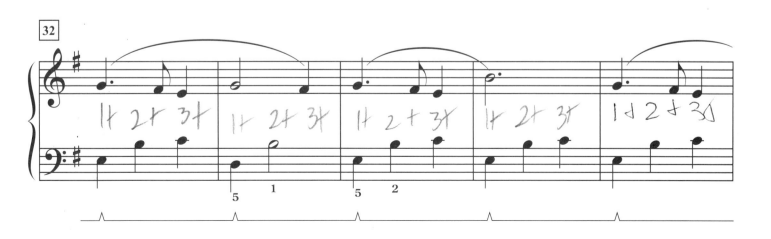

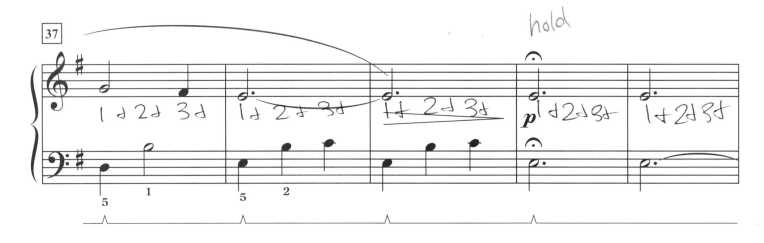

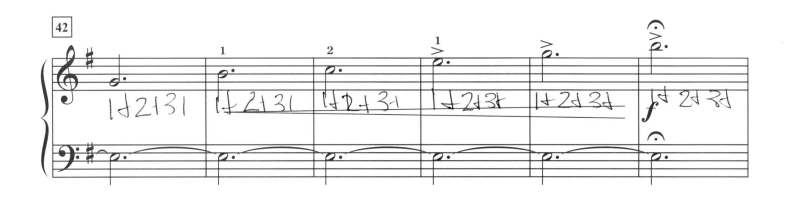

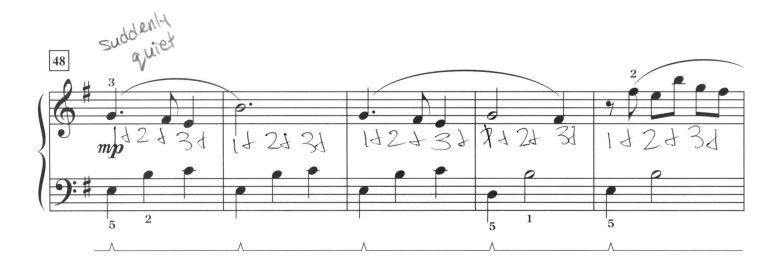

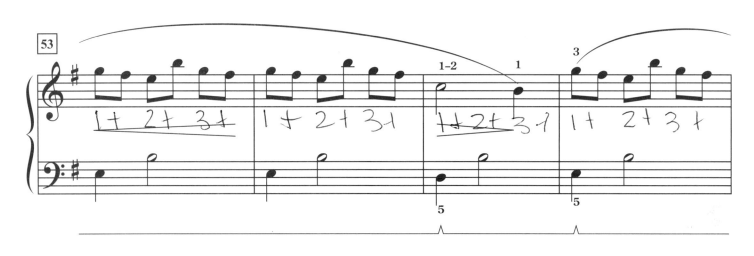

FAREWELL ARAGOG

By Nicholas Hooper
Arranged by Carol Matz

WHEN GINNY KISSED HARRY

By Nicholas Hooper
Arranged by Carol Matz

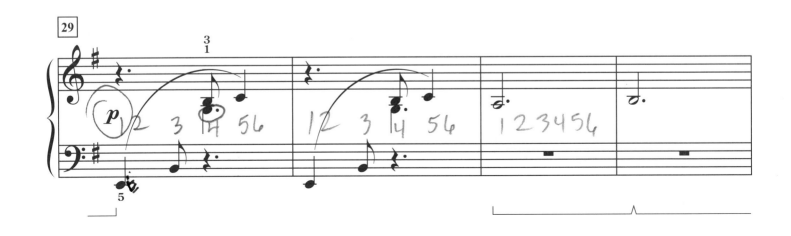

SLUGHORN'S CONFESSION

By Nicholas Hooper
Arranged by Carol Matz

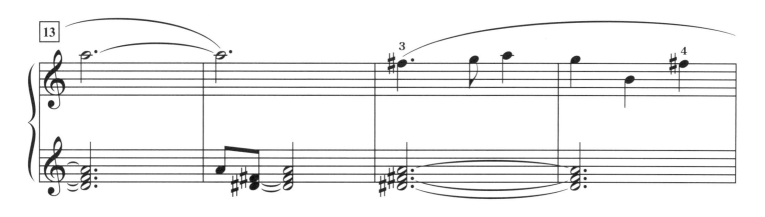

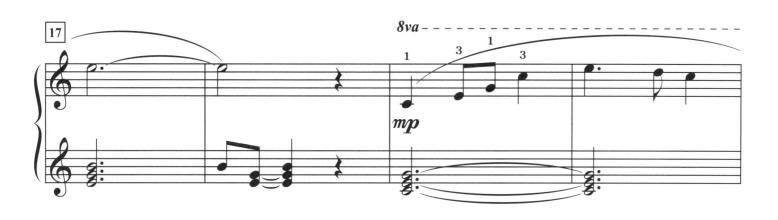

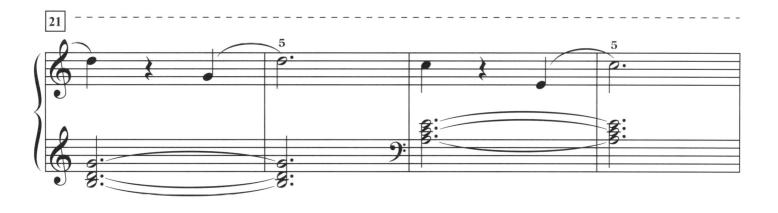

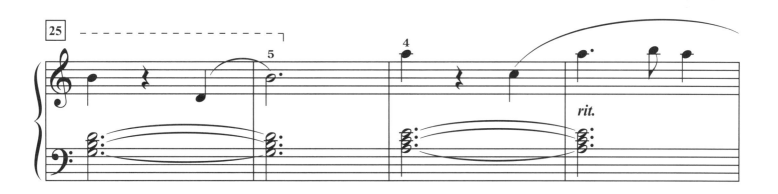

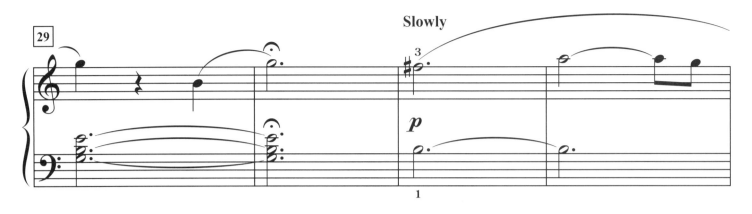

Slowly

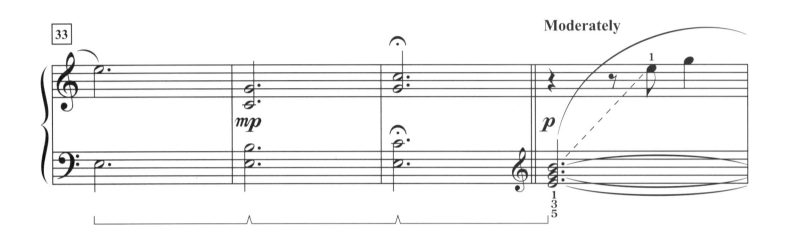

Moderately

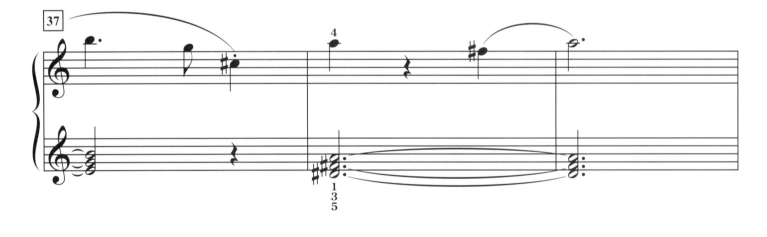

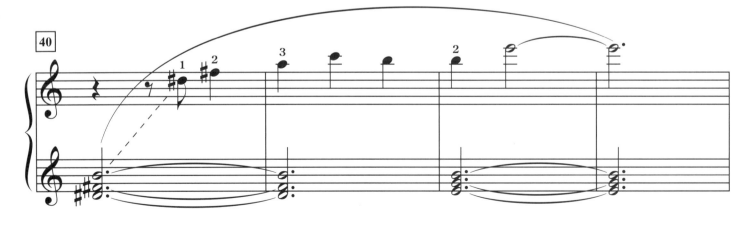

Slowly, freely

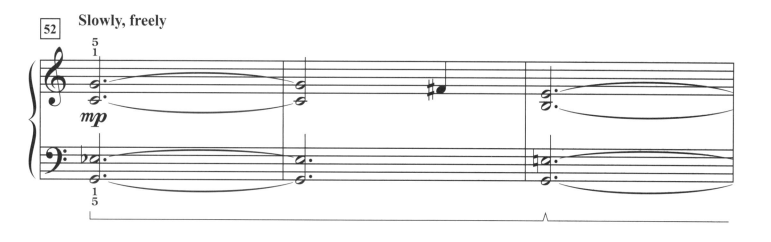

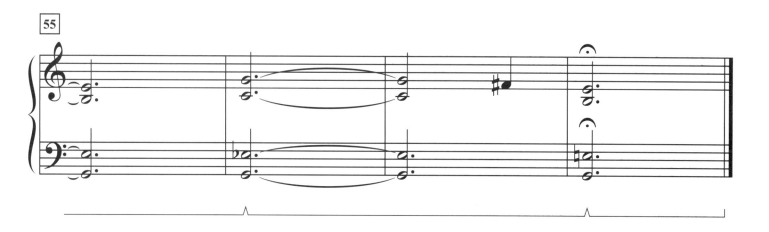

DUMBLEDORE'S FAREWELL

By Nicholas Hooper
Arranged by Carol Matz

Moderately slow

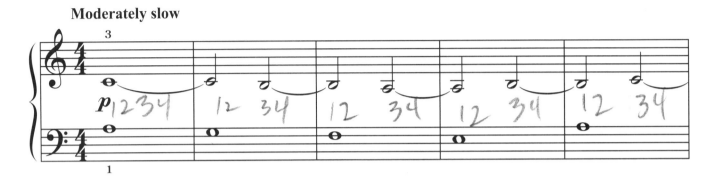

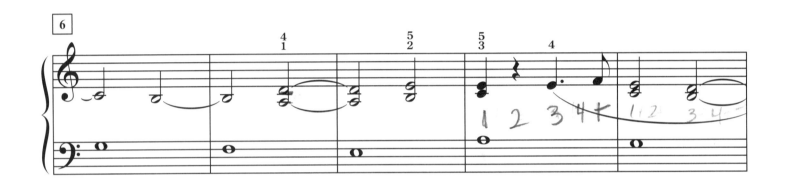

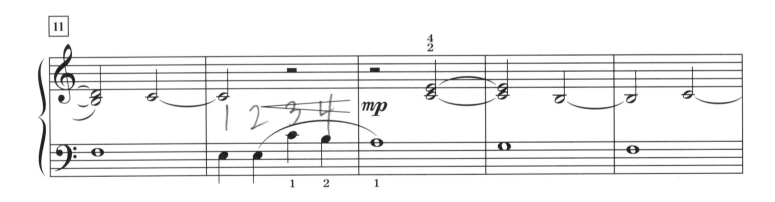

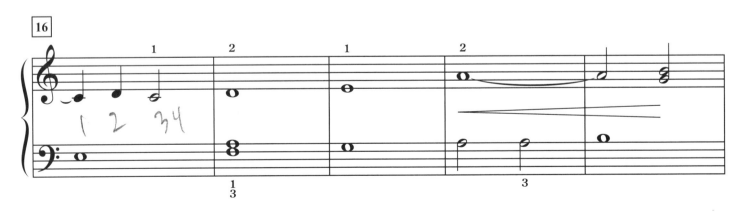

get louder

loud   get softer

THE FRIENDS

By Nicholas Hooper
Arranged by Carol Matz

Moderately slow

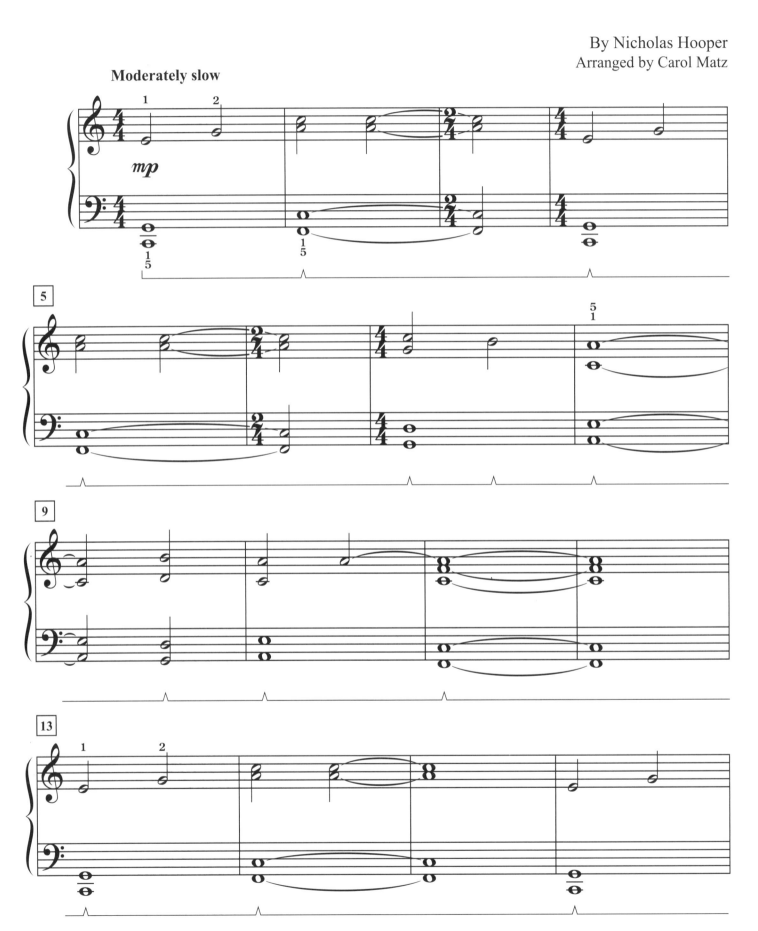

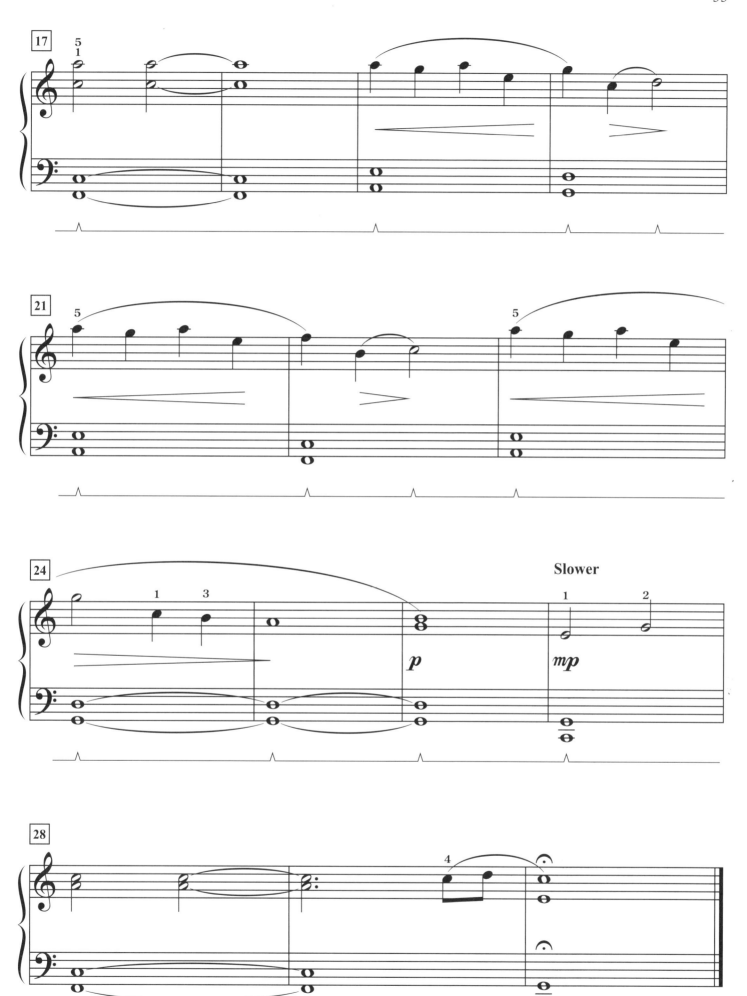

THE WEASLEY STOMP

By Nicholas Hooper
Arranged by Carol Matz

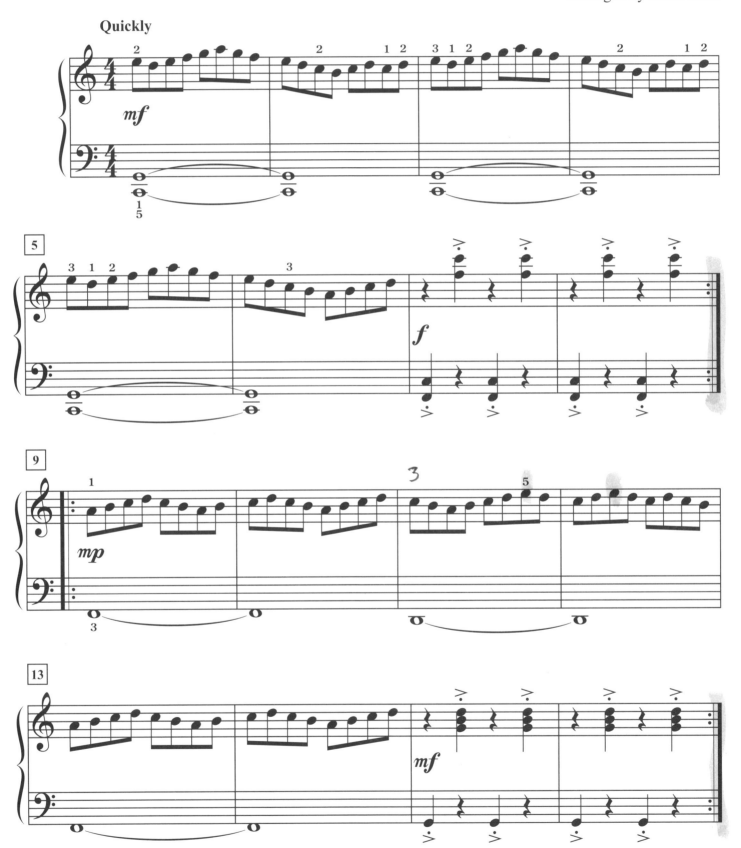

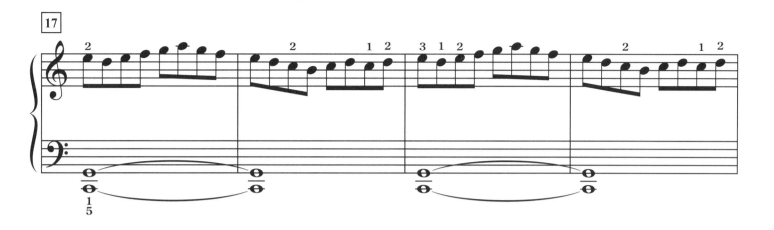

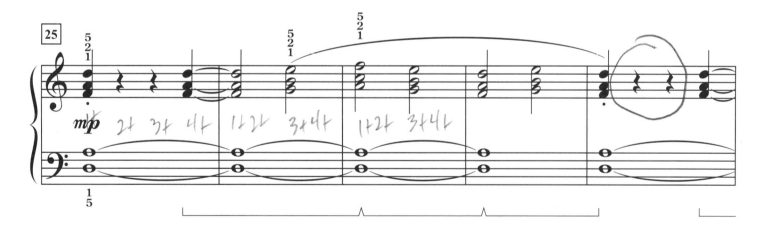

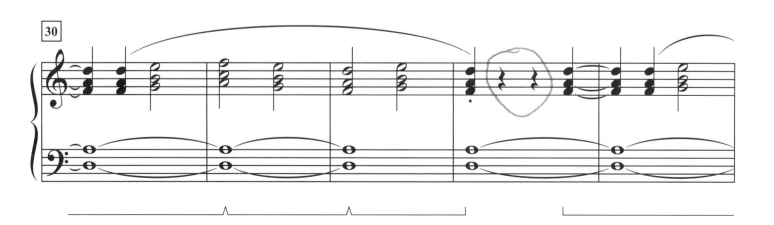

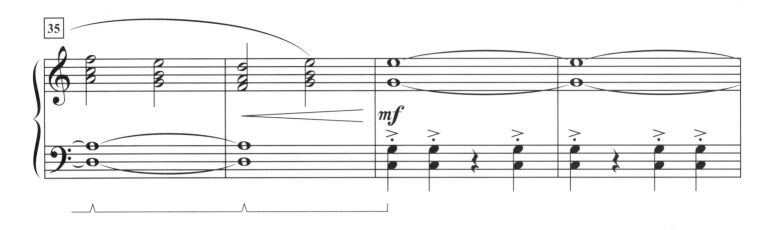

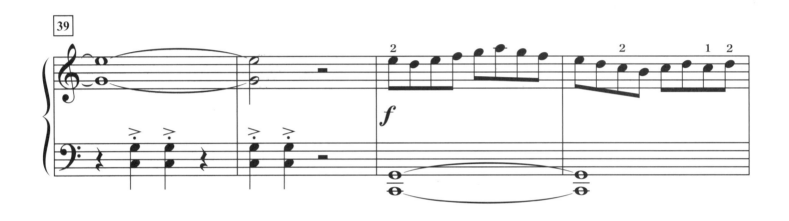

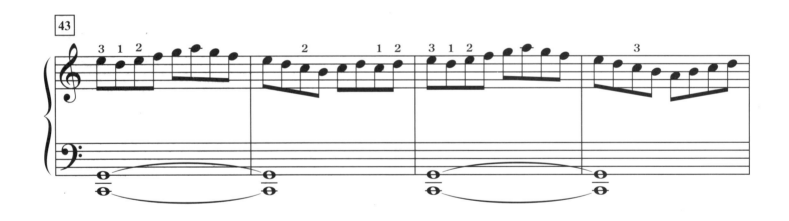

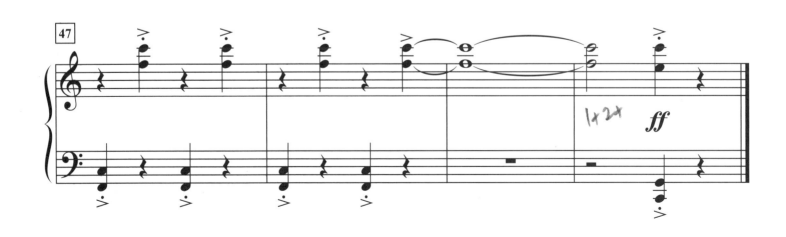